RK LAXMAN

(1921–2015)

Edit: Abhilasha Aggarwal
Design: Subhasish Munshi, Balkishan Verma, Jitender Kumar
Cover design: Subhasish Munshi
Production: Neeraj Bharti

An Uncommon Man – RK Laxman
©Bennett, Coleman & Co. Ltd.

Published in 2015

Published, Marketed & Distributed by

(A division of Bennett, Coleman & Co. Ltd.)
Times Annexe, 9-10, Bahadur Shah Zafar Marg, New Delhi-110002

Printed at
Lustra Print Process Pvt. Ltd.

ISBN: 978-93-84038-67-0

Price: ₹499

Contents

A cartoonist enjoys not a great man but a ridiculous man.

— RK LAXMAN

Introduction

RK Laxman slew a thousand giants in his daily cartoons. Brutus from William Shakespeare's *Julius Caesar* was not one of them. But, arguably, he took very seriously the Roman's injunction on how to assassinate the good and the great: "Let us carve him as a dish fit for the gods, not hew him as a carcass fit for hounds." This was the unique genius of the man. His favoured weapon was the stiletto, not a sledgehammer. His barbs hit home with gleeful precision, but he never covered his targets in blood.

Laxman was internationally feted, a national treasure, but he was nurtured, revered and admired most of all at the Times Group, his 'home' for 68 years. Yes, he was sometimes sworn at for his exasperating arrogance (but always softly and well out of his hearing). His corner office on the third floor of the heritage building, facing Mumbai's Chhatrapati Shivaji Terminus, remained a shrine even after he chose to go and live in Pune, where he had built a house for himself. Purely out of necessity, and perhaps requiring an emergency board meeting, I was assigned this hallowed space when I returned to work at *The Times of India*, Mumbai. There was simply no other cabin vacant. I felt like some crass heretic for removing his angled sketching stand to make place for my computer on that formidable desk. His beloved crows on the shimmering peepul outside the scenic window cawed their protest at my temerity. For the entire time that I occupied that cabin, RK Laxman's burnished brass nameplate remained on the heavy teak door.

Laxman joined TOI in the year of India's Independence; he passed away to the strains of the national anthem closing the 66th anniversary of Republic Day. In those momentous decades, Laxman immediately cut to size anyone and everyone who presumed to think he or she was above the Constitution. And, of course, he did it his way — never pompously, certainly never viciously or even maliciously — but leaving the message unequivocally clear. He did it with humour, finesse and with an awesome economy of strokes.

Laxman was a diminutive man. But he dwarfed everyone else in media. Not just other cartoonists, but journalists as well. With that one 'You Said It' cartoon in just one column square, he managed to encapsulate all that writers need many lines and columns to express. Henri Cartier Bresson said a great photograph captures the 'decisive moment' but a Laxman cartoon captured the 'decisive mood' of the day.

It wasn't just his years of experience as a cartoonist that enabled him to deliver the *coup de grace*... it was his schooling in life, his jawdropping ability to capture expression or even a stance with such frugality came from his keen observation, starting perhaps from infancy. By the time he was four, he was already capturing the wily crow that was to become almost as much of his signature as the iconic 'Common Man'. The little boy's mother was pleased by this fascination because the crow is the mount of the Hindu pantheon's equivalent of Saturn, and she thought it would ward off any evil eye cast on her precocious son. An older Laxman would have responded with his usual dismissive "Nonsense, I zay". For him, the bird outsmarted, out-mooded humans.

Laxman passed away at a time when the thinking world was in the grip of the L'affaire *Charlie Hebdo*. The immediate shock of the killings of cartoonists and others at the controversial French satirical magazine led people, including world leaders, to proclaim solidarity by saying "Je Suis Charlie, I am Charlie." But on cooler thought, some publicly but many privately changed that to "Je Suis Stupid". In upholding freedom of expression, can one be crassly insensitive? For Laxman, this was a non-issue. In that vast corpus of cartoons, there's not one that crosses the line of decency which in itself is an amazing achievement.

Again, as a mark of the unique genius of the man, his cartoons remain uncannily relevant even decades after they were crafted. This is not because politicians, poverty and potholes have remained the same but because Laxman had the extraordinary capacity to drill down to the core of the issue and fathom the depths of public response. 'You Said It' was exactly what you and I would have said if — and that's a big IF — we had his singular ability of expression. His alter ego may have been the Common Man, but his talents were anything but common.

Of course, it wasn't just his daily pocket cartoon... his three-column political cartoon was up there on Page 1 every Sunday. His cocky crows apart, he loved sketching Ganesha, and he had a large portfolio of drawings, all evocatively detailed.

What was it like to work with Laxman? Well, no one really worked with him. He worked in solitary splendour. And no one simply dared to 'drop into' his office. Not even the editor. And, you must remember, the editors of those days were the Zeus in Mount Olympus, Indra in Mount Kailash.

Laxman came to work dot at 8.45am, parked his black Ambassador in his reserved slot closest to the side entrance of the heritage building, and marched into his office with his black briefcase. He did not ever used any of the flashier wheels that had zoomed into a liberalized India. He replaced his car every five years — with another black Ambassador. His sartorial style was as unchanging... in the office at least. He was never seen in anything but a short-sleeved, white, cotton bush shirt and black trousers.

The Edit meeting was at 10 every morning. By then, Laxman had more or less formulated the next morning's cartoon in his head. Before he actually put sketch pen to paper, he knew not just the theme, but the architecture of the composition, the graph on the wall, the squiggles on the curtain, the way the main character would be standing or sitting, the flunkeys around him or her, and, of course, the position of his eternally quizzical Common Man.

So, did that humble icon always look this way, with his trademark *dhoti*, checked long coat and gravity-defying dual tufts of hair sticking out from the sides of his head? Hearsay has it that he first wore trousers, and then evolved to this form. Once set, he never changed his clothes, his hairstyle or his expression. And he never spoke a word in the nearly 70 years of his existence. Like ordinary common men, he suffered in silence. Or was too dumbstruck by the venality, audacity or sheer stupidity of those who fancy themselves as *netas*.

The one time when Laxman himself withdrew into silence was during the Emergency (1975–77). He refused to draw at all rather than subject himself to the Censor. And, on the rare occasion that he went out during those years, he made it a point to introduce himself as a 'plumber' or similar nonentity.

Towards the end of the 1980s, the editor and his elite corps of edit-writers had moved from Bombay to Delhi along with the corporate headquarters. Laxman had refused because he guessed, quite correctly, that being so close to the seat of power might compromise his criticism, blunt his edge. And Laxman being Laxman, no one could order him to go to Delhi, or even suggest that he do a rethink.

Laxman made no bones about the fact that his colleagues had been towering intellectuals, Sir Francis Lowe, Frank Moraes, NJ Nanporia, Sham Lal and Girilal Jain, and how he now had to "suffer pygmies such as you lot". But he would occasionally deign to drop by at our own editorial meetings and disrupt it with his anecdotes about past editors, politicians and the more pompous of guys from *the other side*, that is management. How could we complain about this delaying the start of our day's writing? The stories were riveting, recounted with dry humour by a man who had rubbed shoulders with the likes of Bertrand Russell and TS Eliot, whose brother was RK Narayan (of *Malgudi Days*), and who had caricatured just about every leader of the 20th century... Attlee, Churchill, Hitler and, of course, the Indian political pantheon.

Up there, I am sure, he's probably not sparing even God.

BACHI KARKARIA

Bye-lateral Relations

Excellent news! With these we can aid some more neighbouring countries and improve our ties!

Good Times, Mad Times

BACHI KARKARIA

Off the page too, Laxman was a laugh riot who cracked TOI journos up with his mimicry and deadpan wit.

His iconic status may have been drawn from his 'Common Man', but Laxman's signature feature was a complete absence of the common touch. Why would he bother with mortals? He was genuflected to by all our secular gods, and he had walked amidst a pantheon of legendary editors, starting with Sir Francis Low.

By the time I entered the hallowed precincts of *The Times of India* edit conference in 1989, he graced it only as a favour. The editor and his inner circle had shifted to Delhi from Mumbai some years earlier. Typically, Laxman had refused to budge; he rightly argued that proximity to the political powers would blunt his rapier's edge.

He would condescend to regale our awed assembly with stories of the grand old days, told with droll deadpan wit. If he was in an exceptionally good mood, he would wind up the tale with one of his coin tricks. That's why his trademark white bush shirt had those deep, low pockets.

Even less known than his sleight of hand with coins was his fantastic gift of mimicry. The target of his perfectly pitched imitations would usually be the self-important personages from the 'other side'. Laxman belonged to the era of the unbreachable 'wall' between editorial and management.

Laxman's stories always extended the conference time, so I never managed to put them down. Regrettably so, because when I began writing a book on the 'mythology' of TOI a few years ago, Laxman had already suffered his first stroke and he could not, or would not, recall all that rich lore.

He did, however, mention how Bertrand Russell told him "Indians have discovered nothing" and quickly added with a twinkle in his eye "Don't look so angry, young man. I meant they are the ones who discovered the concept of zero."

Or how Sir David Low, arguably the 20th century's greatest political cartoonist and caricaturist, had one day walked into Laxman's cabin in the *The Times of India* and said "I loved your work right from the days you drew for *The Hindu*. I am on my way to Hong Kong, and I simply had to stop by in Bombay to meet you."

Laxman recalled "I took him to Malabar Hill, and showing him the sweep of grand buildings along Marine Drive, patronizingly said 'You fellows think India is only a land of snake charmers.' Just then, we heard the strains of a pipe, and there was a snake charmer!" Laxman also met TS Eliot, and that was "arranged through Graham Greene, a friend of my brother" — the celebrated novelist RK Narayan. When you are yourself a name, who dare accuse you of dropping them?

Did Laxman ever have a serious quarrel with any of the Indian editors with whom, incidentally, he was designated on par — Frank Moraes, NJ Nanporia, Sham Lal, Girilal Jain? "Never. We held each other in great respect. Frank was a fine gentleman. Yes, sometimes a bit high." Was it true that he would come into office reeling, and write his most hard-hitting editorials when drunk? "Nonsense, I zay, that is all nonsense," spluttered Laxman, his trademark disdain not in the least softened by the 2003 stroke.

When Mumbai was still TOI's editorial and corporate HQ, Laxman, by virtue of his elevated position in the hierarchy, would sit at the outer edge of the edit conference's mystic semi-circle arranged around the quasi-divine editor, Girilal Jain. Because he was out of Giri's line of sight, and more so because he was Laxman, he would sit through all this, pulling faces and imitating the editor as he lit his pipe and made his *ex cathedra* pronouncements. The rest would find it impossible not to crack up, let alone concentrate on the complex theories being expounded.

Dileep Padgaonkar's impressive postprandial repertoire has several Laxman stories. On a trip to Patna together, the iconic cartoonist was mobbed by crowds. He adored the adulation, but then got vastly irritated.

He tried to wriggle out of the last exhibition he had to inaugurate, but the eager organizers said "Sir, please, it will be over in five minutes." Laxman turned to Dileep and hissed "I zay, nothing in this country is over in five minutes. But watch me."

He cut the ribbon and whizzed out saying something to his taken-aback hosts. To a bemused and impressed Dileep, he confided "I zimply told them 'Not today, not today. Today's my Wednesday vow.' In India, the safest way to escape is by using religion."

Once Gautam Adhikari drove Laxman from Boston to New York. "I have never had such a side-splitting four hours in my life. At times I had to pull the car off the highway and stop, I was laughing so hard," he recalled. Along with stories, jokes and gossip, Laxman went into a routine about an air accident that morning, in which the roof had mysteriously blown off. With a completely straight face, he described how the plane suddenly became a convertible, what happened to the air hostess as she was pouring the tea, etc. etc. — periodically shaking his head and saying "It's sad. Very sad."

By the time I returned to the Mumbai office of TOI in 2005, Laxman had 'retired' to Pune, and his cabin was the only one available. It was daunting to occupy that formidable shrine into which no one other than The Editor had ever dared to enter without a summons; for the record, it continued carrying his name for the 18 months of my tenancy — and for four years thereafter. Outside stood a giant peepul, its glistening leaves ablaze in the afternoon sun. On it, the crows, which Laxman had immortalized almost as much as his common man, performed their riveting, cocky, cacophonous choreography.

Looking out of Laxman's window at this scene, I would feel an eerie connect, more humbling than mystic.

I had spent 35 years in the profession, but those months in his absent 'presence' drove home the chasm between being good and being a genius. I could sense Laxman sneering loftily in agreement.

I do not remember wanting to
do anything else except draw.

— RK LAXMAN

Democracy on Death Row

Get on with the preparations. There is no need for you to remind me about austerity — I've been observing it every year for 10 years!

Yes, you are right, the Kamaraj plan is a big failure... look at the way we are fighting still!

This is all I could grab today!

We will call for a bigger total bandh! We will allow not only milk supply, the press and hospitals to function but also schools, offices, shops, transport...

... I have repeatedly told you that poverty must go and yet nothing has been done about it....

Janata will not break up, because... because it is..., I mean it has... well, it won't... break up....

In death of Laxman, India will miss the genius who made the common man into a national icon.

— PRANAB MUKHERJEE, PRESIDENT OF INDIA

Life and Times of RK Laxman

Born in the then Mysore on 24 October, 1921, RK Laxman was the youngest of six sons of a school headmaster and was the younger brother of the famous novelist, RK Narayan. This noted cartoonist, who would later go on to earn a legendary status as the creator of the iconic Common Man and for his pointed satirical cartoons had shown sparks of his brilliance from a very early age. A keen observer of people and things, a young Laxman would doodle and scribble human figures and forms, drawing inspiration from the mundane and the ordinary. Laxman was engrossed by the illustrations in magazines such as *The Strand Magazine*, *Punch*, *Bystander*, *Wide World* and *Tit-Bits* even before he could read. Soon he was drawing on his own, on the floors, walls and doors of his house and doodling caricatures of his teachers at school. Praised by a teacher for his drawing of a peepul leaf, he began to think of himself as an artist in the making.

Another early influence on Laxman were the cartoons of the world-renowned British cartoonist, Sir David Low (whose signature he misread as 'cow' for a long time) that appeared now and then in *The Hindu*. Laxman noted in his autobiography, *The Tunnel of Time*, "I drew objects that caught my eye outside the window of my room — the dry twigs, leaves and lizard-like creatures crawling about, the servant chopping firewood and, of course, the number of crows in various postures on the rooftops of the buildings opposite".

After high school, Laxman applied to the JJ School of Art, Bombay, hoping to concentrate on his lifelong interests of drawing and painting, but the dean of the school wrote to him that his drawings lacked "the kind of talent to qualify for enrolment in our institution as a student" and refused admission. He finally graduated with a Bachelor of Arts from the University of Mysore. In the meantime, he continued his freelance artistic activities and contributed cartoons to *Swarajya* and an animated film based on the mythological character of Narada.

Laxman's earliest work was for newspapers and magazines such as *Swarajya* and *Blitz*. While still at the Maharaja College of Mysore, he began to illustrate his elder brother RK's stories in *The Hindu*, and he drew political cartoons for the local newspapers and for *Swatantra*. Laxman also drew cartoons for the Kannada humour magazine *Koravanji*. Laxman also held a summer job at the Gemini Studios, Madras.

But the rejection at JJ School during his teenage days always gnawed. And years later, the cartoonist in his quintessential Laxman-esque manner wrote "I was grateful to the dean who had administered the JJ School years ago for rejecting my application. If I had been accepted and had graduated clutching a diploma in Arts, perhaps I would not have become the cartoonist that I had become; I would most likely have been languishing in some corner of an advertising agency, drawing visuals for mosquito repellants or pretty faces for ladies cosmetics, or chubby babies to promote vitamin foods, perhaps bearing the name 'Crunchy, Munchy, Vita Biscuits".
His first full-time job was as a political cartoonist for the *The Free Press Journal* in Mumbai, where Bal Thackeray was his colleague. Laxman later joined *The Times of India*, beginning a career that has spanned for over 60 years. His iconic Common Man, featured in his pocket cartoons, was portrayed as a witness to the making of democracy. Anthropologist Ritu G. Khanduri noted "RK Laxman structured his cartoon-news through a plot about corruption and a set of characters. This news was visualized and circulated through the recurring figures of the *mantri* (minister), the Common Man and the trope of modernity symbolized by the airplane".

Laxman's masterstrokes were not restricted to newsprints alone, his work gained popularity in other forms of media as well. Not only did Laxman pen a few novels, he even saw his cartoons appear in films such as *Mr & Mrs '55* (Hindi, 1955) and *Kamaraj* (Tamil, 2004). His creations also include the sketches drawn for the television adaptation of *Malgudi Days*, which was written by his elder brother, RK Narayan, and directed by Shankar Nag. Laxman also drew caricatures of friends for private purposes.

Between 1982 and 1983, when he was visiting Madhya Pradesh as a guest of the then chief minister of MP, Arjun Singh, Laxman captured the natural magnificence that the state had to offer with his deft stroke of brush otherwise reserved to ridicule the vices and follies of the powers that be. There was no pointed satire — a hallmark of the genius — in the exquisite sketches, but only a celebration of the timeless tapestries of nature endowed on the state, which came alive as a book Laxman wrote — *Madhya Pradesh, Random Sketches* with "a few fleeting images left on the eye and not a tourist's guide book". The hill station of Pachmarhi with its waterfalls, pools and serene brooks, the gentle Narmada weaving its way cascading through the marble rocks of Jabalpur, the Jahaz Mahal of Mandu permanently wrapped in sombre atmosphere, the mood of festivity that pervades the whole township of Omkareshwar and the eerie magnificence of Orchha found prominence in his book rather than the quintessential common man of his pocket cartoons. Laxman created multitudinous visages of the common villager from a man sitting on tyre and sipping tea to villagers engaged in cockfight to a gnarled face of a tribal. Even his portrayal of eroticism of Khajuraho was fascinating. Retired Additional Airector, Information & Publicity, Ravindra Pandya, who accompanied Laxman on a 22-day tour of the state recalls, that Laxman was a common man's cartoonist was eloquently proved at Sagar Circuit House when the *khansama* came running to his room with a copy of *The Times of India* to ask whether he drew the pocket cartoon!

In 1954, Laxman created a popular mascot called Gattu for the Asian Paints group when the company wanted to market itself as a brand that was consumer-friendly and reach millions of Indian homes at a time when paints were generally presented as industrial products. The image of a bratty little boy with a wavy tuft of hair clutching a paintbrush in one hand and a can of paint placed next to him had a certain mischievousness about it that caught the imagination of the public and served its purpose — apparently sales soared manifolds. The impact of the ad campaign was such that when years later the mascot was finally dropped from the ad, it is said that the top management from the company felt compelled to visit Laxman to personally explain their reasons.

Laxman's stint with advertising doesn't end here. At one time, Air India had approached him to give his rendition to their famous 'Maharaja' mascot. In more recent times, one can think of his association with Air Deccan, another airline carrier looking at middle-class India as their target group flyers. And in came Laxman's Common Man (with a little knapsack on his back) as the brand icon for its low-cost airline. And the taglines on offer ranged from 'Of the people, for the people, by the people' to 'India's Common Man has a plane to catch' and 'Now everyone can fly'. Clearly, the aim was to find a connect with the Indian masses and get the newly emerging aspirational middle-class hooked to flying. When you wish to position your brand as people's airline, what better way than to have the 'common man' on board?

As an acknowledgement of his vast oeuvres, Laxman was conferred with Padma Vibhushan in the year 2005. Besides, he was also honoured with Ramon Magsaysay Award for Journalism, Literature and Creative Communication Arts in 1984. He was given Lifetime Achievement Award for Journalism by CNN IBN TV18 in 2008. As a testimony of tribute to this cartoonist, there is a chair named after RK Laxman at Symbiosis International University.

Coming to his personal life, Laxman was first married to the Bharatanatyam dancer and film actress, Kumari Kamala Laxman. The couple had no children together. After they were divorced, Laxman later married a lady whose first name was again Kamala. This was the authoress and children's book writer Kamala Laxman. The couple had a son named Srinivas. In a cartoon series named 'The star I never met' in the film magazine, *Filmfare,* he painted a cartoon of Kamala Laxman, with the title 'The star I only met!'

Surely wit, satire, and humour were synonymous with this legendary cartoonist who breathed his last on 26th January 2015, at the close of India's Republic Day. The man may have left us, but the legend lives on.

Kuch Kuch Locha Hai

Beautiful packing ... we've made it at last! Now we must try to manufacture some goods to put in it!

It's a disastrous step! But a bold one! I welcome it!

Here is an interesting deal, Sir. This backward nation is willing to give us everything we want soap, baby food, bread in return for the know-how for a nuclear blast.

Just whose clever idea is this. Putting a milk bottle along with the relics of ancient civilization?

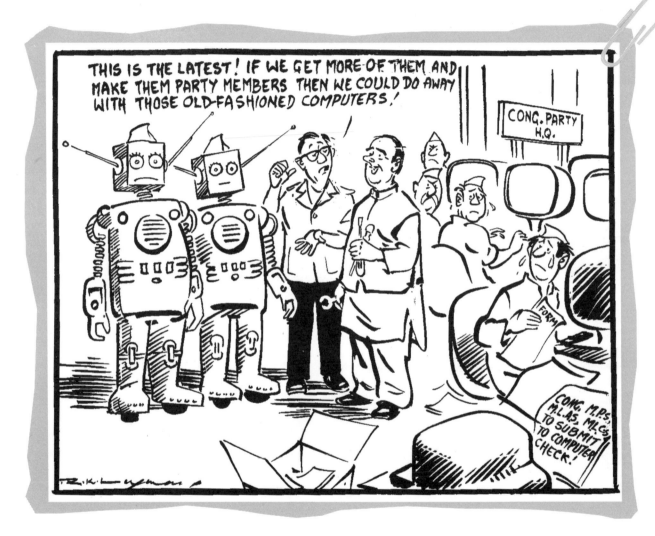

We will say that we will gladly give him support while continuing to oppose him and also try toppling him without removing him from leadership.

Crows are so good looking, so intelligent. Where will I find characters like that in politics?

— RK LAXMAN

Being Irreverent
Faith in laughter, laughter in faith

JUG SURAIYA

The many tributes that were paid to *The Times of India* cartoonist, RK Laxman, when he shed his earthly vestment to be reborn in the *avatar* of his immortal 'Common Man' had one thing in common: They all remarked on his uncanny ability to balance a lively irreverence with a total absence of malice. This is the real secret of his art, which will continue to live on after him.

The distinction between 'irreverence' and 'malice' is of particular relevance today when the world stands deeply and bitterly divided between those who champion the cause of freedom of expression, as represented by the French satirical magazine, *Charlie Hebdo*, which lampooned Islam and the Prophet, resulting in the death of 13 people, and those who believe that matters of religious faith are sacrosanct and beyond the purview of scepticism and humour.

Such confrontations have taken place earlier, most notably in the case of Salman Rushdie's novel *The Satanic Verses*, which resulted in a fatwa being placed on his life. Such face-offs between freedom of expression and the sanctity of religious belief will inevitably become more frequent with the proliferation of social media and the platform for uncensored comment and opinion that they offer.

In a climate in which one man's *bon mot* can be another's blasphemous poison, humour can become a deadly dangerous business. At the core of the problem lies the question: Does humour undermine the transcendent authority of faith?

How can laughter walk the tightrope between irreverence and offence? The clue lies in the equipoise Laxman maintained between irreverence and lack of malicious intent. Irreverence begins by being ready, willing and able to laugh at its progenitors, the satirists themselves. If you can first learn to laugh at yourself, you legitimize your laughing at others, because you have shown that your laughter is not motivated by malice.

The laughter of irreverence is always directed upwards, from a subordinate to an entity of higher status. A joke made by a beggar at the expense of a king is funny; a joke made by a king about a beggar is not a joke but malicious cruelty. That's the paradox of irreverence: By its very nature it also subsumes an upside-down reverence. If we laugh at that which is deemed superior to us, we ratify that superiority by our laughter.

An example of such reverent irreverence — or irreverent reverence — is the Indian custom of referring to God by the familiar form of address, *tu*, which is used for children, those of a lower social status and lovers. If our God can't stand a bit of kidding at His cost, then He doesn't deserve to be our God, worthy of our worship.

The laughter of irreverence sans malice is laughter directed not at someone or something, but laughter with everyone and all things, including divinity and the concept of divinity itself. Jean-Paul Sartre called genius "the scandalous audacity of nothingness". The genius that we call laughter has the same negative capability: it can mock all of creation because it has first mastered mocking itself.

That's the gift of laughter, one that we can share with — who else? — the 'Common Man' and all humanity.

Netas in the Net

You don't have to leave in order to form an anti-Congress party.
You are allowed to stay on and do it!

If he attempts again, that would be really his bye-bye election!

...or maybe people want to suffer under a non-Congress government instead of under a Congress government!

The hall looks empty because everyone wants to sit on the dais, Sir.

Laxman's Tryst with MP in Random Sketches

PARTHA MAITRA & ANKUR SIROTHIA

Legendary cartoonist, RK Laxman captured the natural magnificence of Madhya Pradesh with his deft stroke of brush when he was the state guest of the then Chief Minister, Arjun Singh, between 1982 and 1983. There was no pointed satire — a hallmark of the genius — in the exquisite sketches, but only a celebration of the timeless tapestries of nature endowed on the state. This was collated into a 140-page book; printed by Thompson Press, Madhya Pradesh; Random Sketches, which Laxman wrote was "a few fleeting images left on the eye and not a tourist's guide book".

Retired Additional Director, Information & Publicity, Ravindra Pandya, who accompanied Laxman on a 22-day tour of the state said, "He would tell me that images are embedded in his mind and he could reconstruct them any time. He was a humble, simple man who would be awake at dawn and start sketching even when most of the world was asleep."

Laxman found Pachmarhi more attractive than all other hill stations due to its profusion of waterfalls, pools and serene brooks and was particularly fascinated by the gentle Narmada weaving its way majestically between tall marble rocks of Jabalpur, he said. The quintessential

'Common Man' of his pocket cartoons is missing in the sketches, but rather he created multitudinous visages of the common villager from a man sitting on tyre and sipping tea to villagers engaged in cockfight to a gnarled face of a tribal. Even his portrayal of eroticism of Khajuraho was fascinating.

"Laxman would come and go during his more than a year-long tryst with Madhya Pradesh. He was fond of PS Dhagat, the then Joint Director of Information & Publicity. And after his book was published in 1984, Laxman enquired about Dhagat and when he heard about his death, he sent a sketch as tribute" said Rohit Mehta, a senior government official.

In the book, Laxman wrote "it will need more than a stub of pencil and a sketchpad to capture the sombre atmosphere that the Jahaz Mahal of Mandu is permanently wrapped up in or the mood of festivity that pervades the whole township of Omkareshwar or the eerie magnificence of Orchha, which has the look of a newly set-up movie prop for shooting some tragic episode in history... a sketch is a pure form of communication between an artist and the subject and his reaction is not cerebral but visual."

That Laxman was a common man's cartoonist was eloquently proved at Sagar Circuit House when the *khansama* came running to his room with a copy of *The Times of India* to ask whether he drew the pocket cartoon, recalls Pandya.

Nothing in my life has been intentional, it's all accident

RADHA RAJADHYAKSHA

Irony was the ink he used to chronicle the political history of India for over 60 years. He gave us the ridiculous side of the most sobering realpolitik and realities, a glimmer of sunshine amid the gloom.

The 'uncommon man' is no more. And with his passing, the curtain comes down on an era of humour that was one of a kind — playful and ironic, astute yet childlike, razor-sharp but malice-free. In a nutshell, vintage RK Laxman.

As a cartoonist who chronicled India's political journey for over six decades, Laxman lampooned virtually every known politician, caricaturing both the emperors in New Delhi and the regional satraps who appealed to his eye for the ridiculous. His eloquent brushstrokes, which captured the quintessence of a personality so amazingly, rendered his caricatures legendary and made for cartoons that could evoke a belly laugh even without the crutch of a punch line (though his verbal lines were as delightful as his artistic ones). His greatest gift, of course, was the 'Common Man', that eternally bewildered symbol of millions of Indians, who looked on mutely as political charlatans and criminals took the country for a ride.

A self-taught artist, Laxman found his calling as early as three years of age, scribbling obsessively over the walls and floors of his Mysore house, despite being "regularly spanked" for it. As he grew older, his talent found an outlet in the local press, where he illustrated, amongst other things, the stories of his famous novelist brother, RK Narayan. Keen on acquiring formal training, he applied to Mumbai's premier art institution, the JJ School of Art, but was unceremoniously rejected on the ground that he "lacked the kind of talent to qualify for enrollment". Laxman didn't particularly care about the snub then; however decades later, he took great delight in pointing this out at a JJ function where he was invited to be the chief guest.

As his magnificent career proved, the lack of academic training didn't turn out to be a stumbling block. Determined to make it as a cartoonist, Laxman left Mysore after his graduation, shuttling between cities and assignments till he landed his first full-fledged cartooning job with *The Free Press Journal* in Mumbai (from where his fellow cartoonist, Bal Thackeray, quit to pursue a more humourless path). After which happenstance and a buggy ride brought him to *The Times of India* in 1947.

In an interview with this correspondent 16 years ago, RK Laxman had outlined the narrative of his tryst with cartooning; how he had begun by accompanying his mother to the market square and sketching anything in sight — a cow chewing, a policeman on his beat, a vegetable seller. "From the beginning, I was fascinated by human figures, the way they stand and sit, the way they lift someone else's hand to check the time and drop it," he'd said. Perhaps it was these exercises in capturing movement, somewhat different from the static model-drawing then practised in art schools, that shaped the amazing fluidity of his cartoons in later years.

Laxman was philosophical, almost mystical, about the circumstances that had led him to don the mantle of India's best-known cartoonist. "Nothing in my life has been intentional," he'd told me. "It's all by accident. I was a humble philosophy-economics-politics student, studying autocracy-plutocracy-democracy; banking-currency-inflation; Vedanta-Plato-Socrates. Where did cartooning come in from? From the very beginning, why did I take such an interest in the tree and how to draw and paint it? Nobody told me to. I used to cycle for miles with my sketchbook in Mysore, which was a very congenial place for an artistic fellow. If I'd been born in Bombay, I think I would have been on the Stock Exchange, Harshad Mehta maybe."

The cartoonist, who'd sketch his teachers in class while the others struggled with arithmetic or grammar, had the gift, he claimed, of seeing a non-human form in every human. "What you see of the face is only a mask," he'd said. "Behind it is an animate object like a tiger or a crow. Sometimes it's also an inanimate object — some people look like broken-down trucks or old buildings. The possibilities are there but you can't see them unless you are slightly mad. You have to have extraordinary vision to see what is going on behind the face that is presented to society."

This ability to perceive a non-human face lurking behind a façade, in combination, of course, with his childlike sense of mischief, is what made Laxman's drawings so delightful and also so unerring. Whether it was the distinctly bovine features of a Narasimha Rao, the eagle-like disdain of an Indira Gandhi, the hint of madness in the sundry politicians, *sadhus* and hangers-on of the '80s-'90s Hindutva brigade, or the permanently fazed expression on the face of the 'Common Man', his caricatures unfailingly captured the essence of a personality. "The caricature is a totally different experience," he'd said. "It is the human face distorted without distorting the personality."

Laxman revelled in this creative distortion — from his early caricatures of Hitler, Mussolini and Churchill ("I must be grateful to them for making me a political cartoonist") to his series on global dignitaries like TS Eliot and Bertrand Russell to Indian film stars (old-timers recall his hugely popular series for *Filmfare* in the 1950s called 'Stars I Never Met'), his brush inked almost every famous face in the world. And then, of course, there were India's politicians, his bread and butter (many, like Narasimha Rao and Laloo Prasad Yadav, he would say were "created for a cartoonist"). Ironically, these targets of his swipes also admired him — if Nehru was a Laxman fan, politicians like Arjun Singh and Jaswant Singh bought his original cartoons and felicitated him. "That's because politicians don't understand cartoons," he'd chuckled when I asked him about this paradox.

It is impossible to say how to become a cartoonist; you have to be born with the gift, just as you cannot tell someone how to sing.

— RK LAXMAN

Queen Empress of India

My common man
is omnipresent.
He's been silent
all these 50 years.
He simply listens.

— RK LAXMAN

Thank you, RK Laxman Sir, for your blessings

RAJESH KALRA

It is not often that you can claim to know, and know well, a real icon, someone you grew up admiring, were always in awe of, someone whose pocket cartoon with a single caption would be a complete editorial, a comment far more effective than 400 plus-word-long editorials we generally utilize to express a strong point of view. RK Laxman was truly a legend, a one-of-a-kind.

As I said, I grew up with his 'You Said It' pocket cartoons. Whenever the newspaper was delivered in the morning (remember, those were the pre-Internet days), irrespective of how big the lead news was, one would scan the entire front page quickly, trying first to get a feel of how the 'Common Man' saw the happenings in the world, and then, once the mood was set, look at the other pages. Imagine my excitement when soon after I shifted base to Mumbai in 1999, for a few months, I realized my cabin was adjoining that of my icon. And that is where my understanding of the man grew. He would often walk into my room and greet lustily. He looked at computers with some suspicion I thought and certainly was in awe of the Internet. Invariably, any chat would veer around the Internet and he would marvel at how what he does can be seen by people all over the world "as soon as you put it up".

His work style was also unique. He would get to work, move around here and there, observing, conversing with some, talking to himself at times. When he talked to himself, it was better to steer clear, for that is when he would be entering into a 'zone'. And little past afternoon, he would be in 'the zone'. He would pick up newspapers, pore over them and then shut himself off from the rest. At this time, you daren't disturb him.

And when he emerged, with him would emerge that day's 'You Said It', the bewildered common man witnessing the acts of movers and shakers and charlatans and lobbyists and all who have messed up India, from close quarters, with a caption that would explain what the man in crumpled *dhoti* and checked *kurta* felt about the action of the big and powerful.

He was a 'Common Man' at heart too. There was one particular period with several close shaves for air passengers. He sauntered into my room and asked: Do you feel scared of flying? When I said no, I don't and that I read newspapers during almost the entire flight duration, he left. The next day's cartoon showed people clapping and wishing each other just because a flight had landed safely, and of course, one man also throwing his newspaper up in the air in excitement, and relief, perhaps! There were also times when he would come in, ask me what I had for breakfast, for I was staying at the office guest house, and tick me off for not looking after myself. I would always smile, feeling elated deep inside for the concern he showed.

Thank you sir, for your blessings!

Sarkari Tarkari

You are shaking all over! Did you come in a taxi ?

There was a leak in the dam. I plugged it by fixing a common water tap !

Don't look at me like that, I am doing my best !

What is this? "We must import sugar, water, vegetables, milk, tea, food..."? When I asked you to think of our long term needs I did not expect you to make a list of this sort!

This is my son. Can he take over? I have reached the age of retirement from service.

Ten years you have taken! I warn you if this building is not completed in another eight years we will have to look for another contractor.

We must demand still bigger pay. What we get isn't enough to see us through strikes like this.

What do you mean, no arrivals or departures? As a government spokesman, you should say they are running according to the revised schedule.

There, Sir! the park we are fighting to preserve. They want to demolish it, cut the tree and make it a car park.

He has been coming for quite some time now, Sir. Seems to be a genuine applicant we would issue him a card.

India will miss you, RK Laxman. We are grateful to you for adding the much-needed humour in our lives & always bringing smiles on our faces.

— NARENDRA MODI, PRIME MINISTER